CANCER IS NOT A DEATH SENTENCE

MICHAEL AND BOBBIE'S HEALING JOURNEY

A Journey of Faith

by

Michael R. Baker

Yattira Publishing
Colorado Springs, CO

Cover Photo by Carly Hartman, www.carlyhartman.com

Cover Design by Satoshi Yamamoto

Edited by Yattira Editing Services
Published by Yattira Publishing
PO Box 26056
Colorado Springs, CO 80936
contact@yattira.com
www.yattira.com

Endorsements

Michael Baker has written more than just a book or Bible study on healing; he has written about his own healing. These are scriptures and principles which worked for him and will work for you. Michael and Bobbie attended the church I pastored in Tulsa, OK and gave of their lives to those who attended. They have always been givers and continue to be so. This book is a gift from Michael to you. It will bless you and others who need a miracle or healing.

Pastor Bob Yandian

Michael and Bobbie Baker made an unlikely move halfway across the country about 20 years ago and ended up in my church. They shared with me that they believed God had brought them to North Carolina as a part of their journey of faith.

I learned that Michael had had a "chance" encounter with the owner of company that sold used electric motors. He offered Michael a job and he took it, even though the new company was one that dealt almost exclusively with "horizontal" motors, and Michael was a "vertical" motor salesman.

As I would soon discover, Michael and Bobbie's mission was neither motors, nor nursing (Bobbie's profession), but serving the Lord as prayer warriors and encouragers. These dear people were at the right place at the right time for me, during one of the hardest ministry seasons of my life, and stood beside me and prayed diligently for me, my family and the church. My wife and I will always be grateful to them.

You will soon understand why the Bakers are such amazing people. This book is a living testimony of faith and prayer lived out through a terrible season in their lives. Thankfully, Michael and Bobbie have decided to share their experience with the rest of us. Page after page demonstrates how followers of Christ can, and should, rely on the promises of scripture, the prayers of other believers, and the Lord himself to orchestrate circumstances for the good of those He loves. This story will encourage you because it is a documentary of God's faithfulness.

As Michael tells his story, he doesn't sugarcoat anything. His cancer was real, and as he ended up in more and more doctors' offices, it became increasingly real. Like any of us would be, he was scared, and his throat cancer was a learning experience of medicines, therapies and radiation. Yet through it all, he and Bobbie put their trust in their Lord and Savior, Jesus Christ. Their Sunday School class prayed, their pastors prayed, their friends prayed, their family (including their grandchildren) prayed, and most of all, they prayed. As much as any medicine, surgical procedure or supplement taken, prayer was the prescription they see as leading to Michael being proclaimed cancer free.

One of the dearest parts of the story to me is that God answered their prayers, right down to the side effects from the chemo and radiation not permanently affecting Michael's health. I praise God that he could go back to work, teach his Sunday School class and even start a new life with a new calling in ministry since the cancer.

Cancer is Not a Death Sentence will encourage you—whether you ever have cancer or not. God has allowed the Bakers to tell us about part of their journey as they struggled with cancer, but all of us will encounter challenges in our lives where we will need to put ourselves confidently in the hands of God to make it through. May this book help you do just that!

Branson Sheets
Lead Pastor
Covenant Church
Greenville, North Carolina

In his new book, *Cancer is not a Death Sentence*, Michael Baker takes you through his personal journey of healing from cancer. In this book, you will see Michael's journey of healing and victory up close and how you too can experience healing. This book is packed with scriptures that contain the seeds of healing and power that brought Michael through his trial with cancer.

Michael will show in this book that God can use doctors and medicine in the healing journey, but ultimately it is God who heals, and He alone is the Great Physician!

Michael also shares the importance of keeping a positive attitude and a sense of humor in our journeys of victory. A merry heart does good like a medicine!

I highly recommend this book to anyone walking through a healing. It is filled with hope, comfort, and spiritual light shining upon the dark path anyone is walking through. As Michael and Bobbie's pastor, I have seen them walk victoriously on the other side of cancer and how their lives are filled with life and ministry to others around them.

If you are struggling with sickness, especially cancer, please read this book! If you know of someone who is walking through dealing with sickness or cancer, please give them this book. It will be a blessing to them!

Rick McFarland
Senior Pastor—River Rock Church
Dean of Education—Charis Bible College Colorado

Dedication

This book is dedicated to the glory of the Lord Jesus Christ our Healer. Let me announce to God Almighty, the Lord Jesus Christ, the holy angels, the devil and his cohorts, that according to the Word of God, I am healed! CANCER IS NOT A DEATH SENTENCE!

Table of Contents

Introduction

"I didn't die. I lived!
And now I'm telling the world what God did."
— Psalm 118:17 MSG

"Faith for the journey of walking with God leads
to encounters with God."
— Bill Johnson

Cancer! Oh no! I'm going to die!

This is what most people think when they hear the word "cancer." Some people experience such fear when they hear that they have been diagnosed, they can't even say the word. They call it the "C" word.

I'm here to tell you that cancer is NOT a death sentence! I'm living proof that you, too, can live and not die and tell others what God has done for you. God does not have favorites! What He has done for me, He can do for each one reading this who believes in Him. This is the story of *our* healing journey.

The reason we titled this book *Michael and Bobbie's Healing Journey* is because cancer affects the whole family. My wife, Bobbie, was as much involved in our journey as I was. Bobbie put her life on hold for me. She went with me to every appointment, radiation and chemo treatment. Not only did she go to my appointments, she scheduled them for me. And when I was unable to drive, she became my chauffeur.

Because she is an LPN, Bobbie understood what the doctors were saying and knew what questions to ask. She made sure I received medicine on time, even in the middle of the night. She patiently and faithfully sat through my two surgeries. For a time, I was unable to eat solid food, and Bobbie changed my dressing to keep the G-tube (feeding tube) free from infection.

Since I had cancer in the throat, there was a period of time when I couldn't swallow, and Bobbie gave me tube feedings five to six times a day. Also, because of her nursing background, it was like having my own private duty nurse 24/7. Taking care of me around the clock took a physical toll on Bobbie, but she continued, day after day, without complaint.

Most importantly, she prayed for and encouraged me. I am so thankful Bobbie was with me every step of this journey. Although the path seemed long and the road hard (it was almost eight months from the time I noticed the lump until I was able to go back to work full-time), God gave us the faith and strength to endure. He will also walk with you every step of the way and give you faith and strength for the journey: you must simply ask Him and believe.

First, I want to make clear that cancer—or any other sickness or disease—is NOT of God. To say that God puts cancer, sickness or any other disease on people is a slap to His face! We live in a fallen world from where sickness comes. Jesus went to the Cross to redeem us from the curse of this fallen world.

In Isaiah 53:5 it is written,

"But He was wounded for our transgressions,
He was bruised for our iniquities;
The chastisement for our peace was upon Him,
and by His stripes we are healed."

Also, in John 10:10 Jesus declared,

"The thief [Satan] *does not come except to steal,*
and to kill, and to destroy. I have come that they
may have life, And that they may have it more
abundantly" (brackets mine).

So, into which category does cancer fall? The *"kill, steal and destroy"* category of Satan, or the abundant *"more abundantly"* life of Jesus? Cancer is a consequence of the door being opened to Satan's influence by mankind's choices against our Creator and His ways.

> *"For the kingdom of God is not*
> *eating and drinking, but righteousness,*
> *peace and joy in the Holy Spirit."*
> — Romans 14:17

> "Since sickness does not bring righteousness,
> does not bring peace, and does not bring joy,
> then it is not of God."
> — Greg Mohr

In 1 John 3:8 it says,

> *"...For this purpose the Son of God was manifested,*
> *that He might destroy the works of the devil."*

Also, Exodus 15:26 says,

> *"...I am the LORD who heals you."*

It does not say, "I am the Lord who puts cancer, sickness and disease on you."

There are seventeen times in the Gospels where it is recorded that Jesus healed all of the sick that were present and forty-seven other times where He healed one or two people at a time. Nowhere in the Bible do we find Jesus refusing to heal anyone. In light of Jesus' statement that He could do nothing of Himself, but only what He saw the Father do (John 5:19; 8:28-29), His actions prove to us that it is always God's will to heal.

So, if you or someone you know believes that God puts sickness and disease on you to teach you something, why would you go to the doctor, or ask for prayer, to get rid of something you believe God gave you? God loves you! Repent for believing a religious lie, and ask God to heal you! He wants you to come to Him and ask. It is His great pleasure to heal you for *your* good and *His* glory.

GOD GETS THE GLORY WHEN WE ARE
HEALED, NOT WHEN WE ARE SICK!

As you take this journey with us, we pray your faith will be strengthened and that you encounter Jesus Christ as the Lord who wants you well and heals you.

Let the healing journey begin...

Chapter 1
The Unexpected Journey

"A journey of a thousand miles
begins with a single step."
– Laozi (Chinese Philosopher)

A thousand miles is not insignificant, and this was a thousand-mile journey that Bobbie and I never expected to take. During our journey, we put a little over a thousand miles on our car traveling from appointment to appointment and from treatment to treatment. Cancer can be a long and exhausting journey. From the first diagnosis, to the operations, to the pretreatments, to the treatments and—finally—to the post-treatments and recovery, over a year or more can transpire.

Thursday, April 24th

The first step of our thousand-mile journey began on a crisp, Oklahoma spring day in 2013. It was a typical day at my job at The Pump and Motor Works. I was an inside technical salesman of used industrial equipment, and I also managed the inventory. A colleague from North Carolina had flown in to help me with the pump inventory to make sure we had all the required information.

As we talked, I made a comment that I had noticed a lump on the side of my neck that morning. He encouraged me to go to have it checked out. He said, "At our age, we shouldn't take anything for granted." Even though I wasn't very old (I was only 55), what he suggested resonated with me.

That night when I arrived home, I told Bobbie about the lump and we prayed. Because I didn't have a primary care physician, the next day, April 25th, Bobbie called a friend, Dr. Michelle Coulter. Even though I was not her patient, Dr. Coulter asked me to come in that afternoon. I left work early and arrived a little after 3:00PM, so I could complete the forms and become established as a new patient.

After she had finished with her scheduled appointments, and everyone but her nurse had gone home for the evening, Dr. Coulter's nurse weighed me. I was shocked. I weighed 262 pounds—the most I had ever weighed! I guess it resulted from a sedentary lifestyle because I sat behind a desk most of the day with very little exercise.

After weighing, the nurse led me to the exam room and charted my medical history and vital signs. Even though I was overweight, my vital signs were normal. After a thorough examination, Dr. Coulter speculated, "It could be an infection, or it could be cancer." She prescribed a ten-day regimen of antibiotics, hoping the lump would disappear, while also suggesting I lose some weight!

Monday, May 6th

During that ten-day period, life was normal. I continued to work, attend church, and spend time with friends and family. Some might call that a boring life, but Bobbie and I considered our life together happy and fulfilled! I started trying to lose some weight, as the doctor had instructed. However, on May 6th, the end of the ten-day round of antibiotics, the lump was still there.

We returned for my follow-up appointment with Dr. Coulter. She was concerned because the lump had not gone away and immediately called a surgeon, Dr. Mark Meese. When she made a same day appointment with him, we knew she thought it was something serious.

After our consultation, Dr. Meese stated, "I want to remove the lymph node and have it biopsied." Surgery was scheduled for May 17th.

As we left his office, Bobbie asked me what I thought, and I declared, "Whose report are we going to believe? We're going to believe the report of the Lord, which says, '...*by His* [Jesus'] *stripes we are healed*'" (Isaiah 53:5, brackets mine).

For the next eleven days we continued to live our normal life. Nothing had changed.

Sunday, May 12th

Sunday, May 12th, we went to church and asked our Sunday School class, *The Dream Team*, to pray for us regarding the surgery, because we knew Jesus declared in Matthew 18:19 (GNT),

> *"And I tell you more:*
> *whenever two of you on earth*
> *agree about anything you pray for,*
> *it will be done for you*
> *by my Father in heaven."*

We prayed in agreement with our class, believing God for a successful surgery, knowing He would guide the hands of the surgeon. We also prayed for Christian nurses, no complications, and a quick recovery. For the next five days leading up to the surgery, Bobbie and I kept praising God. I would spend the thirty-minute drive to the office singing and praising God and the thirty-minute drive back home doing the same. I wanted to keep my eyes on Jesus, not the surgery.

Thursday, May 16th

The day before surgery, we went to Oklahoma Surgical Hospital for my pre-op intake. During that session, as we were talking to the nurse, we began telling her about our faith. She was also a Christian and asked if she could pray for us. As we left, we had such peace knowing that God was going before us.

Friday, May 17th

The day of the surgery finally came. We arrived at the hospital at 6:00AM with confidence, knowing everything was going to be alright. Yet, we wondered why I had to check in so early, since my surgery was not scheduled until 9:00AM. However, while we were waiting to be taken back to pre-op, my son, Chris, his wife Stephanie (whom we call our *daughter-in-love*), and two of our grandchildren came to be with us. It was comforting knowing the family would be there with Bobbie during my surgery, so the extra time was good!

Finally, the nurse came to take me back to the pre-op room. While Bobbie and I waited in pre-op, our dear friend, Cheryl, arrived to meet with us, along with one of the staff members of our church. They encouraged us and prayed. We have been so thankful to have had supportive, loving people with us every step of the way.

When the time came for the surgery, everyone was asked to go to the waiting area, and I was wheeled to the operating room. As they were preparing me, Dr.

Meese came in and asked how I was doing. I replied, "Fine," and with that, they put me under anesthesia.

The surgery only lasted about thirty minutes and was without any complications, just as we had prayed. While I was taken to recovery, Dr. Meese talked to Bobbie. He explained, "The lump looked like a normal cyst that he's probably had since birth."

After a few hours in recovery, I was released to go home. We felt good about the doctor's report. Once again, we went back to life as normal, not knowing how much our normal life was about to change!

Wednesday, May 29th

On Wednesday, May 29th, we returned for our scheduled post-op visit to have the sutures removed. Dr. Meese explained that in the center of the biopsied node, "The lymph node had *dead* squamous cell carcinoma." Bobbie and I believed since the tissue was black and the blood supply cut off, Jesus had healed me. Still, Dr. Meese ordered a PET scan.

Bobbie called my mom to give her the doctor's report. We asked her if she would come to the house and pray with us. Thank God for praying moms! My mother came, and we had a powerful time of prayer—God showed up! Mom laid hands on me, and her prayer was so powerful, my body started to shake. Initially, she saw darkness in the spirit realm, but then she saw light come and knew I was going to be alright.

The same afternoon, Bobbie called Kellie Yandian with the report. Kellie arranged for her husband, Pastor Robb, herself, and Brian Booth (a board member and good friend of mine) to pray for me after Wednesday night service. They laid hands on me, and we believed, once again, in the healing anointing of our God and Father of Heaven.

The Bible tells us in James 5:14-16 (NLT),

> *"Are any of you sick? You should call for the elders of the church to come and pray over you, anointing you with oil in the name of the Lord.*
> *15Such a prayer offered in faith will heal the sick, and the Lord will make you well. And if you have committed any sins, you will be forgiven.*
> *16Confess your sins to each other and pray for each other so that you may be healed. The earnest prayer of a righteous person has great power and produces wonderful results."*

When they were finished praying, Pastor Robb said, "After God heals you, you need to shout it from the rooftops." I assured him that I would! This book allows me to "shout it from the rooftops," and tell what God has done for me!

Friday, May 31ˢᵗ

Two days later I had the PET scan with a CT X-ray, and then went home for a nice quiet weekend to wait for the test results. At that point, we didn't realize we had only taken a few steps of our journey. We had no idea how busy our lives were about to become and went to church on Sunday, as was customary. Not very many people knew what was going on with us; we had only told a few close friends and family who we knew would stand with us in faith and continuously speak positive words. We did not want people who were in fear speaking negative words over me.

Tuesday, June 4ᵗʰ

On Tuesday, June 4ᵗʰ, I saw Dr. Atul Vaidya, an ear, nose and throat doctor. He scoped me (he put a small camera through my nose and looked at my throat) and said he couldn't see or feel anything, but the PET scan showed cancer. The primary site was on the right side, at the back of my tongue. He referred me to Dr. Scott Cole, an oncology doctor at the Tulsa Cancer Institute, and warned me I would probably need chemotherapy and radiation.

However, we still thought it was stage one and could probably be treated with good nutrition and prayer. The appointment with the oncologist was made for Wednesday, June 12th.

However, after returning home from the appointment with Dr. Vaidya, Bobbie's nursing instincts kicked in, and she researched oral cancer. At the time, Cancer Treatment Centers of America did not have an ear, nose and throat specialist, and they did not accept our health insurance. Bobbie also checked MD Anderson's website in Houston and discovered that the typical treatment for oral cancer was six to seven weeks of radiation and chemotherapy. We now had a good idea of what our journey might look like!

Seven weeks from the time I noticed the lump, we still had only a speculative diagnosis. However, we knew when we saw Dr. Cole that we would have a definitive diagnosis. Sometimes waiting can be the hard part. During this time, I chose to keep busy by focusing on Jesus and continuing to work. The time went by quickly, and the day arrived for my appointment.

Wednesday, June 12th

Dr. Cole reviewed the PET scan with us, and Bobbie asked him if this was stage one. He said, "No, due to the size of the lymph node, it's *stage four!*" He recommended a treatment of "The Big Guns"—radiation and chemotherapy—for six to seven weeks. He also made a recommendation for me to see a nutritionist. Actually, Bobbie had already made that appointment for the next day. The Lord was leading and guiding us every step of the way. Dr. Cole told us that the next day,

Tulsa Cancer Institute would be moving to a brand-new building with state-of-the-art equipment.

While he was talking, I thought, *Throat cancer? I can't have throat cancer! I can't have radiation to my throat! I need my voice! I'm a salesman! I talk for a living!*

I had also taken a class at church entitled *Called to Teach*, so I could help teach Sunday School. *What am I going to do if I can't teach?* I thought. As I was thinking these things, the Lord spoke to me and said, **"Cancer is not a death sentence. You will not die, but live, and declare the works of the Lord"** (Psalm 118:17). Instantly, supernatural peace came over me, and I knew everything was going to be alright.

Yes, God still speaks today.

In John 10:27 Jesus said,

> *"My sheep hear My voice, and I know them, and they follow Me."*

So how did God speak to me? No, it was not in an audible voice. One of the ways God speaks to us is through His Word, which is the Bible. He spoke to me by bringing Psalm 118:17 to my remembrance.

That night at church, Pastor Robb said, "If anyone is sick, come forward for prayer." I immediately responded. The Lord spoke through Reverend Geof Jackson, **"He is fighting the battle for you, Michael! Just like He fought the battles for the children of Israel."**

"Every battle is won or lost before it's ever fought."
– Sun Tsu, The Art of War

CANCER IS LIKE A BIG BULLY, AND JESUS
IS OUR BIG BROTHER.

Jesus defeated cancer over 2000 years ago on the Cross, so we don't have to fight this battle. God is good.

We knew this battle was won before we ever started. When you put your trust in Jesus, He keeps you in *perfect peace*, for the Bible says,

"You will keep him in perfect peace,
Whose mind is stayed on You,
Because he trusts in You."
– Isaiah 26:3

We had no fear or anxiety because we knew this battle was already won. As we kept our eyes on Jesus and His Word, we had that *"perfect peace."*

Someone once said,

"Feed your faith and
your fears will starve to death."

How do we feed our faith? **By focusing on the answer to our situation and NOT the situation itself.** The answer to our situation is God's Word.

The next day, I shared with Bobbie my real concern, which was finances. How were we going to make it if I couldn't work? Also, my second concern: Who was going to mow the lawn? Mowing the lawn may seem a small thing, but it was heavy on my heart because we lived in a subdivision with covenants regarding keeping your lawn neat.

I went to my job at The Pump and Motor Works that morning and talked to my boss about the test results. He assured me my job was secure and asked what I needed. He told me the main thing was, "...to get you better." I told him I was concerned about paying our bills!

Since Bobbie had "retired" shortly before this, it took both my salary and a commission to meet our budget. He asked how much the budget was and when I told him, he responded, "Don't worry about it. We will cover it. Let us know if you need anything else." He even went as far as to bring my paycheck to me while I was going through treatment. The financial burden was miraculously lifted!

The same day I had talked to my boss, Bobbie also shared the test results with one of our friends from Sunday School. The same person later called back and said, "God has laid it on my heart so strongly that the

18

Sunday School class can mow your lawn for you. We will take turns every week."

Some of you reading this may not realize what a sacrifice of love that was. Summers in Oklahoma can be brutally hot. Wow! We didn't even need to ask, and God took care of my concerns. God is concerned about even the little things that concern us.

The Bible says,

"The Lord will accomplish what concerns me."
– Psalm 138:8 NASB

Thursday, June 13th

That evening we went to see our friend, Lorrie Medford, who was a registered nutritionist, just as Dr. Cole had instructed us. She was pretty amazed that we had already changed our diet to a healthy one months before, but suggested supplements to build up my body before starting chemotherapy.

Friday, June 14th

The next day, June 14th, we were off to another appointment. This time with Dr. Meese's associate, Dr. Griffin. To prevent repeatedly being poked with needles, he said I needed a chemo port in my upper chest to provide access to a vein for chemotherapy. Also, he explained I needed a G-tube (feeding tube) in my stomach for nutrition, as I would be getting radiation to my jaw and neck. I ended up being so thankful I had the G-tube, because my throat became burned through the radiation treatment, and I was unable to swallow anything after a few weeks. Following this consultation with Dr. Griffin, surgery was scheduled for June 18th.

Sunday, June 16th

The Sunday before surgery, I went up for prayer, and God gave Reverend Geof Jackson another word for me: **"The healing has already begun,"** which was an answer to a previous prayer for a quick healing! Five months (from the time I had my first treatment until I was back at work) may not seem like a quick healing, but as far as cancer battles go, it was. After that word, I went upstairs and taught our Sunday School class.

When I was finished teaching, we made the announcement of the diagnosis the doctor had given us. The entire Sunday School class laid hands on me and prayed over me again. There is so much power in agreement! (When we finally received a definite diagnosis, we started telling people about it, so they could stand with us in prayer.)

By this time, our faith was built up and we were confident that God was fighting the battle for us; we were no longer worried about people speaking doubt and unbelief. When I told a really good friend about the diagnosis, I could hear the fear in his voice. When he said, "I'm so sorry," I sensed he believed I was going to die.

Only because my faith was built up was I able to encourage him and say, **"Cancer is not a death sentence. I'm going to be fine."**

Monday, June 17th

The next day, June 17th, we returned to Oklahoma Surgical Hospital for another pre-op intake. This was required because this surgery was a month and a day from my last surgery. I was told if surgery had only been scheduled the day before, I would not have had to go through intake again. However, God's hand was even on this. We had a Spirit-filled pre-op nurse, and God used *us* to encourage *her* in a personal situation she was going through at that time.

Tuesday, June 18th

The following day, June 18th, again we were required to arrive early for surgery. Dr. Griffin put the chemo port in my left upper chest and the G-tube in my stomach. The surgery went well with no complications. Afterward, they took me to the recovery room where the nurse was a believer in the Lord Jesus Christ and was walking through some very difficult times of rejection. Both she and her husband were in ministry, yet God used us to shine light into her darkness. Speaking the truth of God's Word to her gave her the hope and encouragement she needed at just the right time!

Even while walking through what appeared to be a difficult situation, we found it possible to be an encouragement to others. We don't have to allow circumstances to dictate how we feel. We need to keep our eyes on God and not on our problems.

Wednesday, June 19th

Wednesday, June 19th, and it was another day, another appointment, as we continued along this unexpected journey's path. On this particular day, we were on to an audiologist because I was told I needed a hearing test, as the chemo drug could affect my hearing. However, we also began to believe this would not occur!

We chose to believe what the Bible declares:

"No weapon formed against you shall prosper..."
– Isaiah 54:17

As with any long journey, there are times you need to stop and "take a break." The following week was a break for us. We had no appointments, so we were able to take it easy, and I was able to work remotely from home for a couple of days.

On Saturday, *The Dream Team* Sunday School class had a scheduled get-together and barbeque at a friend's home. Because I was able to rest for a few days, I felt able to go. It was great to relax and be around friends. While I was visiting with people, the mother of a friend who was visiting from Arizona started talking with me. As I shared with her what was going on, she asked if she could pray. She laid hands on me and prayed, believing God for my complete and total healing. She told me she felt the power of God go through her fingers. It was so good to be surrounded by loving and praying friends.

The next day at church, during Sunday School class, we had another visitor whose friend was dying of liver cancer. I prayed for his friend, the same thing God had spoken to me, "**Cancer is not a death sentence and it will not win.**" This was another opportunity to get my eyes off my own situation and be an encouragement to someone else.

Looking back, I probably overdid it at the barbeque; after church, I had to go home to rest and take some pain medicine. I needed all the rest I could get because we had a busy week ahead of us.

And so, the journey continued...

Chapter 2
Doctors Treat but Jesus Heals

"People of faith have a higher survival rate than those who don't have faith." – Mackie Sutton, Physician's Assistant

"It is reasonable to expect the doctor to recognize that science may not have all the answers to problems of health and healing." – Norman Cousins

Wednesday, June 26th

On Wednesday, June 26th, we hit the ground running, as we had three appointments scheduled. Our first appointment was with Dr. Cole in the new, state of the art Tulsa Cancer Institute facility. The facility was amazing, and the people were friendly and professional.

The first person we met was Shelby, one of the receptionists, who was so nice and pleasant. Every time we arrived for an appointment, Shelby always had a smile on her face and a kind word to share. Because many patients arrived with a "doom and gloom" attitude, I'm sure she had learned to make the day a little more pleasant for them. We didn't always look forward to the treatments, but we always looked forward to talking with Shelby. After a few weeks, whenever she saw us she would come around her desk and give us a welcoming hug.

When we checked in, we went upstairs to see Dr. Cole. His nurse weighed me before I was seen by Dr. Cole, and I weighed 242 pounds. Praise God! I had lost twenty pounds in nine weeks! We knew that "doctors treat, but Jesus heals," so we needed to determine whether I would receive treatment or believe God for healing. We decided to do both. I knew I was not alone. I went through the treatments with Jesus' healing power walking through them with me. We knew every one of our doctors was handpicked by God!

While we were meeting with Dr. Cole, Bobbie said, "You know, doctors treat, but Jesus is the Healer." He responded, "Yes, I know I can't heal anyone." This was our confirmation that Dr. Cole was exactly the right doctor for me. You see, some doctors have an attitude of pride and superiority, as if they are God, but Dr. Cole understood he was the doctor, but Jesus is the Healer.

Our visit with Dr. Cole was more routine than anything else. He wanted to know how I was doing and if I had any questions or concerns before we began. I said I was fine and ready to get started with treatments. Because I had not seen a radiologist, the doctor's opinion was that it would be a couple of weeks before I started receiving treatments. Once treatments began, a firm schedule would be set.

After we left Dr. Cole's office, we immediately went downstairs to see Dr. Nguyen, a radiologist. We were blessed because both doctors were in the same building. Originally, I had been referred to another radiologist, but had not had a good feeling about him. He was with another doctor's group. So, when we saw Dr. Cole on the twelfth, we told him about my apprehensions. He said there was also a radiologist with their group of doctors, so Bobbie called and made an appointment with Dr. Nguyen, instead. We know God had His hand on this, also. Conveniently, we were now able to access both doctors because they belonged to the same doctor's group.

Dr. Nguyen examined me and then did a scope, putting a camera through my nose to look at my tongue. Again, there were no visible signs of cancer. However, she had the disk of my PET scan and showed Bobbie where the cancer was located. Dr. Nguyen took her time and went over the treatment and explained all the potential side effects that could come as a result.

We were believing God that none of these side effects the doctors mentioned would manifest, including:

- sores in the mouth in week three
- skin reaction turning skin red
- fatigue
- low blood count
- difficulty swallowing
- dry mouth
- loss of taste
- loss of teeth
- risk of hypothyroidism
- loss of hearing
- stroke

God supernaturally protected me from all of these side effects, because we believe:

"No weapon formed against [me] *will prosper..."*
– Isaiah 54:17 (brackets mine)

We appreciated Dr. Nguyen's compassion along with her honesty. After she explained these possible reactions, she said I would need a mask for the radiation treatments to protect the parts of my body that didn't need treatment. She told us her office would call to schedule the appointment.

Following our appointment with Dr. Nguyen that day, we headed to our third appointment. We had been so busy, we had not taken time for lunch; even then, we were running late for the next appointment, my post-op exam with Dr. Griffins. He was the doctor who had put in my chemo port and G-tube.

After his examination, Dr. Griffins reported that things were "looking good," and he wanted to see me again on Friday, July 5th, to remove the supports on the G-tube. He told us, "I like to keep them in (the supports) for at least two weeks."

By the time we left his office it was 4:00PM; we still hadn't eaten, and we were really hungry. We wanted to be at church by 6:00PM to meet a friend who was willing to help us set up our page, *@MichaelAndBobbie'sJourney*, on Facebook. I heard the Lord speak to me about this Facebook page. I was to chronicle our journey for other people to help and encourage them.

When we left Dr. Griffin's office, we immediately stopped for something to eat, then went home to let out Ivory, our golden-doodle dog, before we headed to church. We made it to church right at 6:00PM. Because our day had been so hectic, after church we went directly home and right to bed.

Thursday, June 27th

After having three appointments on Wednesday the 26th, we thought Thursday the 27th would slow down some. That was not the case. When the radiologist said she would get back with us to schedule the appointment, she was serious. We already had an appointment at 11:00AM to see Lorrie Medford, our nutritionist. Dr. Nguyen's office called at 9:00AM and said they wanted us there at 11:00AM.

We changed our appointment with the nutritionist and instead went to Dr. Nguyen's office where they did a CAT scan to mark me for my radiation treatments. They also made a mask to fit my face that would help protect the areas that didn't need radiation. The mask had to be made before I could start any treatment. Dr. Nguyen explained, "The mask must fit tightly, so I can radiate the exact spot each time." She did not want me to lose any more weight.

Now, I had gone from being happy, because I had lost twenty pounds, to being told I should not lose any more weight. Little did I realize at the time how difficult it would be to keep my weight on.

Next, it was on to our appointment with the nutritionist. She was having me take nutritional supplements to get my body built up before I started treatments. After our appointment with Lorrie, we had to return to Tulsa Cancer Institute in time for the class on chemotherapy. It started at 5:30PM and we arrived at 5:29PM! (I know we are supposed to obey the speeding laws, but I won't tell if you don't!)

This class described what to expect and was very informative; we received many helpful tips. The one I really didn't like was learning I would have to use an electric razor! Even though I would lose the hair on my head, the instructors assured me I would not lose my beard or mustache. I decided to shave off my beard and mustache and go for the "Kojak" look. We left class at 7:00PM and rushed to a *Graceful Ladies* meeting, a women's group that was an extension of our church. At the time, my wife was on the leadership team of the group and had to be there. (I so appreciate my wife and all she does!)

Friday, June 28th

The next day, Friday, June 28th, we left for Lincoln, Nebraska, so Bobbie could visit her family before the treatments began. I wanted to do that for her because of what she was getting ready to go through in supporting me in the days ahead. Dr. Cole thought it was okay for us to travel, since we weren't scheduled to start treatment until July 8th. We took our five-year-old granddaughter, Samantha, along with us.

We had originally planned a trip in August to celebrate Bobbie's mother's 89th birthday, but with treatments five days a week, that was not going to be possible. We had a good visit, and we were able to meet Bobbie's great-niece for the first time. Bobbie was thankful for that. On the last day of our visit we had a "mini" family reunion with twenty-three of her relatives joining us at a restaurant, since we knew it would be a while before we would see them again. Everyone had a good time.

That night, when we went to bed, Samantha wanted to say the prayer. Of course, we let her, and her prayer was precious. She prayed, "Jesus, heal my Papa because I want to play with him. Jesus, heal him." Then she looked at us and stated with confidence, "He [Jesus] said, 'Yes.'"

Wednesday, July 3rd

We returned from Nebraska to Tulsa on the 2nd of July. The day before, we had received a call from Dr. Nguyen's office, asking me to come to the radiology class on Tuesday. (As I said before, they move fast!) We told them we would not be available until Wednesday the third. They informed us that because July 4th was a holiday, classes would not resume until Tuesday, July 9th. The timing seemed strange to us because I would have had two radiation treatments by then.

However, we knew God was going through these treatments with me, so I had nothing to fear. One of the words from God we were standing on was Isaiah 43:2 (NLT, brackets mine), which the Lord had spoken to Bobbie:

"When you go through deep waters,
I will be with you.

When you go through
rivers of difficulty,
you will not drown.
When you walk through the
fire [radiation] of oppression,
you will not be burned up;
the flames will not consume you."

Here is another word from God upon which we were standing:

"The Lord is my shepherd;
I shall not want.
He makes me lie down in green pastures.
He leads me beside still waters.
He restores my soul.
He leads me in paths of righteousness
for his name's sake.
Even though I walk through the valley
of the shadow of death,
I will fear no evil, for you are with me;
your rod and your staff, they comfort me.
You prepare a table before me
in the presence of my enemies;
you anoint my head with oil;
my cup overflows.
Surely goodness and mercy shall
follow me all the days of my life,
And I shall dwell in the house
of the Lord forever."
– Psalm 23 ESV

We had confidence God was with us through each step of the journey, including this part, just as He had been with us every step so far.

On Wednesday, July 3rd, we hit the ground running, again. We saw another nutritionist, because my doctors wanted me to see one associated with their group, who also had offices in the same building; it made our lives a little easier. This nutritionist wanted me to have between 2800 and 3000 calories a day. (I thought that wouldn't be hard for someone like me who likes to eat.) I was told patients typically lose about twenty pounds during radiation, and they were trying to prevent that from happening in my body.

After leaving the nutritionist's office, we drove across town to see my dentist, Dr. Bracken Fennel, because the radiologist explained that I might lose my teeth. My dentist said he would work me into his schedule, but when I arrived, he had already received a cancellation, so I got right in. After examining my teeth, Dr. Fennel said I only needed one tooth build up before radiation. He also explained I would need a tray for fluoride.

Dr. Fennel told us that a previous patient, with the same type of cancer diagnosis as mine, had used the fluoride tray and did not lose any teeth. I thought, *Not only will I have the fluoride tray, I will have God on my side.* I was believing God for two angels with flaming swords to protect me, just like those in the Garden of Eden. The dentist wanted me to have my teeth cleaned, because once treatment started, no invasive treatments would be allowed. (God is so good! He had already made a way for me to be seen by Dr. Fennel; He knows what we need before we know and already has the answer!)

When we left Dr. Fennell's office, we had some personal things to attend to, with not much time to spare with so many appointments. I dropped Bobbie at the store and hurried home to let Ivory out and feed her. She knew something was going on, because she didn't leave my side. Whenever we would leave the house, Ivory would act depressed. After I was done taking care of her, I returned to pick up Bobbie. It was now 6:50PM, and we headed directly to church.

The church was having a fireworks display, so after the service, we stayed around to watch the show. They were a good distraction. We sat with our *Dream Team* Sunday School class. Bobbie and I also sat with Brian and Cheryl, the friends I previously mentioned, who were getting ready to travel to Europe for vacation. Cheryl mentioned that if I changed my mind about getting chemo, Bobbie and I could join them for vacation. *Let's see, go through chemo, or go to Europe?* Yeah, I had to think about that one! However, I knew God was leading me to do the chemo, so I stayed to go through the treatments.

After the fireworks, Gabriel, our four-year-old grandson who had come along, wanted to come home with us. Since we had taken his sister, Samantha, to Nebraska with us, we were happy to have him spend the night. We knew once the treatment began, I would be quarantined for some time. As we were getting ready for bed, Gabriel watched Grandma (Bobbie) change my feeding tube dressing and told me he wanted to pray for me. Gabriel prayed the most simple, pure, childlike prayer over me, *"Jesus, heal my Papa's belly owie."* It was such a blessing for two of my grandkids to pray for me.

Thursday, July 4th

On July 4th, we took it easy. We went to my brother's home for a family BBQ. I was in some pain, so I sat by the pool and watched the kids play. It was nice just to relax. We were so exhausted from all the running we had been doing, we left earlier than we normally would have. Once home, we were in bed by 8:30PM!

Friday, July 5th

We woke up on Friday and prepared to go to an appointment at Dr. Griffin's office to have the stitches removed from supports on my feeding tube. We were relieved to have only one appointment on the schedule. *Yay!*

We finally received a call from Tulsa Cancer Institute with my treatment schedule. I was instructed to arrive at 8:15AM on Monday the eighth, for lab work. I was then scheduled for my first chemo treatment (they said it would last about four-and-a-half hours), followed by my first radiation treatment. They explained I would have chemo every Monday at 8:30AM.

As I arrived for my first treatment, the Lord brought to my remembrance Mark 16:18:

"They will take up serpents; and if they drink anything deadly [chemotherapy drugs], *it will by no means hurt them..."* (brackets mine).

God also reminded me of the story of Shadrach, Meshach and Abednego, found in Daniel chapter three. They were thrown into the fiery furnace, but Jesus was in the fiery furnace with them and protected them.

I knew Jesus would protect me from the fire of radiation and chemo.

On Monday, the "real" journey would begin.

Again, knowing I would be quarantined and unable to have any visitors, we wanted to see the grandkids one last time before treatments began. Grandma Bobbie picked up our other two grandkids, Mackenzie and Brandon, while I stayed home and rested. We had a family photo made with all four grandkids, along with one son and daughter-in-love, before all my hair fell out. Mackenzie and Brandon spent the night and went to church with us that next morning. It was so good to spend some time with them. After church, we took them out for pizza and to the park, and then we took them home. Mackenzie and Brandon expressed their concern for me, and we told them I would be okay, because Jesus was with me and would take care of me.

Monday, July 8th

The day of the "real journey" finally arrived. As usual, it was a sweltering hot day for July. Even that early in the morning the temperature was rising rapidly. We arrived at the Tulsa Cancer Institute around 8:00AM.

Shelby was there with her warm smile to check us in. At 8:20AM, I was taken to the lab to have my blood drawn, then upstairs to see Dr. Cole's physician's assistant, Mackie Sutton.

When we had finished with Mackie, we were taken to the chemo center. We learned Dr. Cole and Dr. Nguyen had agreed to change my chemotherapy treatments from seven small doses once a week to one large dose every twenty-one days for the best results.

At 9:50AM, the nurse started an IV with plain fluid. Then at 12:05PM, the nurse began my first chemo treatment. While I was receiving the chemo, we were informed the brand-new radiation machine was not working properly and was being repaired. They re-scheduled the radiation to begin the next day. We definitely didn't want a machine that wasn't working!

We finally finished the chemo treatment at 3:10PM. We had been there almost seven hours for the first treatment. Everybody who worked at the chemo center kept telling me I would get nauseated, but we were believing God that wouldn't happen. We asked people to pray in agreement with us that there would be no nausea.

We know the Bible declares,

"Again, I say to you that if two of you agree on earth concerning anything that they ask,
it will be done for them by My Father in heaven."
– Matthew 18:19

After we left TCI, we went to the pharmacy to have five prescriptions filled; three of which were for nausea. One of the miracles Bobbie and I were trusting God for was that I wouldn't have any nausea, period. Now it was time to rest and be ready for my first radiation treatment the next day.

Unfortunately, that night was a rough one. I was so tired, but my body would not slow down. I was "buzzing" all night long. We suspected it was from the chemo drug. Around 9PM, I took four milligrams of Valium, but it did not help. When Bobbie got home from class, I told her what was going on. She took my temperature, which was normal, but my heartrate was 104. We were supposed to call the doctor if my temperature was over 100.5, because the chemo drugs kill off good cells along with the bad.

Bobbie gave me Phenergan for nausea, but I didn't want to take it **because I wasn't nauseated**. She told me it would help me sleep. By the time morning had arrived, I had only slept a total of maybe four hours.

One of the effects of chemo is "chemo brain." Everything becomes fuzzy, it seems like you move in slow motion, and everything you do is a chore. Yet, we had a busy day ahead of us: dentist appointment, radiology class, and my first radiation treatment.

Because it was such a rough night, I woke up with "chemo brain." I wanted to "dress for success" for my first radiation treatment, so, to prepare, I decided to put on the armor of God.

"Put on all of God's armor so that you will be able to stand firm against all strategies of the devil.
12For we are not fighting against flesh-and-blood enemies, but against evil rulers and authorities of the unseen world, against mighty powers in this dark world, and against evil spirits in the heavenly places.
13Therefore, put on every piece of God's armor so you will be able to resist the enemy in the time of evil. Then after the battle you will still be standing firm.
14Stand your ground, putting on the belt of truth

and the body armor of God's righteousness.
¹⁵*For shoes, put on the peace that comes from the*
Good News so that you will be fully prepared.
¹⁶*In addition to all of these, hold up the shield of faith*
to stop the fiery arrows of the devil.
¹⁷*Put on salvation as your helmet, and take the sword*
of the Spirit, which is the word of God."
– Ephesians 6:11-17 NLT

Here is how I put on my armor. First, I put on the *helmet of salvation*, which is the Word of God; I would shelter my mind from Satan's attacks of doubt, depression and discouragement by keeping my eyes on Jesus, and His Word, rather than the treatment ahead of me.

Next, I put on *the breastplate of righteousness*. Since my own righteousness was but filthy rags (Isaiah 64:6), and Jesus has clothed me with the robe of His righteousness (Isaiah 61:10), I had confidence to come boldly to the throne of God and make my requests known (Hebrews 4:16). I knew that when God looked at me, He saw Jesus' righteousness in me. I then put on *the belt of truth*, which is the Word of God that says by His stripes I was healed (1 Peter 2:24).

Next, I put on the *shoes of peace* because the Word of God says:

"You will keep him in perfect peace,
Whose mind is stayed on You..."
– Isaiah 26:3

After that I took *the shield of faith*, which quenches all the fiery darts of the wicked one (Ephesians 6:16).

And lastly:

> *"Then your salvation will*
> *come like the dawn, and your*
> *wounds will quickly heal.*
> *Your godliness will lead you forward,*
> *and the glory of the LORD will*
> *protect you from behind."*
> – Isaiah 58:8 NLT

I was confident that as I went forth, the Word of God would go with me. God confirmed this truth, because before we left for Dr. Fennell's office to pick up the fluoride trays (I wanted to use them before my first radiation treatment to help protect my teeth), I received an email from some friends. They sent me a healing scripture for the day that helped me combat the "chemo brain":

> *"...As for you, I'll come with healing, curing the*
> *incurable, Because they all gave up on you*
> *and dismissed you as hopeless..."*
> – Jeremiah 30:17 MSG

From Dr. Fennell's office, we traveled back across town to TCI for our 12:30PM radiation class. Then I waited on the machine for my radiation treatment. The staff was running behind schedule, since the machine hadn't been working on the previous Monday. After waiting, and waiting some more, I was finally taken back for my treatment. They allowed Bobbie to go back with me, so they could also explain the process to her. This was also an opportunity for Bobbie to take some great pictures for our Facebook page describing (what we were confident would become) our healing journey!

First, technicians had to line me up on the radiation machine and Dr. Nguyen had to approve the alignment. After her approval, the radiation treatment began. The alignment took about twenty minutes, but the actual radiation treatment only lasted 292 seconds.

After the treatment, I was slated to visit further with Dr. Nguyen. As became our *new normal*, you guessed it, there was more waiting! This treatment process reminded me of my time in the military: *Hurry up and wait!* Bobbie had an appointment at 3:30PM (life must go on), so she had to leave me there to get to her appointment on time.

When I finally saw the doctor, she said everything was fine, but my liver enzymes were a little high. Even so, Dr. Nguyen didn't seem to be too concerned. By the time Bobbie returned and we made it home, it was 5:00PM. I was so worn out, I went straight to bed and slept for 90 minutes.

The next day, the waiting continued! Even though TCI was a new, state-of-the-art facility, one of the drawbacks was that they hadn't yet worked out all the "kinks." When we arrived for my 8:30AM treatment on Wednesday, we were informed that the radiation machine was down again.

The staff guessed it would be working again in about an hour, so we chose to wait. Yet, one hour turned into two, which turned into three. Unfortunately, we had not prepared to be there as long as we were. Since the doctors didn't want me to lose any weight, I not only needed to eat something every couple of hours, but I had to take my meds as well. However, we had not brought my medication or food!

We learned a valuable lesson that day: we never left the house without carrying some food and my meds. Finally, after four hours of waiting patiently, I asked how much longer it would be and was told it would not be ready until the next day! We were told to call before we came in on Thursday to be sure the machine was working.

Bobbie was concerned about the fact that I hadn't eaten in a very long time, so we left right away to get some lunch. Again, I was so tired that when I got home, I went straight to bed.

A couple of hours later, the treatment center called and told us the machine was working and I could return if I wanted. I told them I was too tired. In a way, my decision was a good one because that night I had enough energy to go to church.

Since we were told Wednesday afternoon that the machine was working, we got ready for our 8:30AM appointment. Bobbie tried to call before we left but was unable to get through. So, as we were driving, I finally connected and—you guessed it—the machine was still down. We had to reschedule for 3:30PM that afternoon. It really didn't bother me too much, because, as I mentioned before, I didn't want a machine administering radiation that was not working properly.

After the treatment, we decided to get my hair cut off before it fell out. After we arrived home, I shaved off my goatee and mustache. I was going for the "Kojak" or "Mr. Clean" look. Bobbie told me I looked different, but I was the same Michael and was still telling jokes. I told Bobbie, "If I have to go through this, I might as well have fun."

Praise God! When I went in for my next treatment, the radiation machine was working. Finally, after four days, they got all the "kinks" worked out.

As I prepared to start another week of radiation, the Lord gave Bobbie a scripture passage, Philippians 4:5-7 (NASB):

"Let your gentle spirit be known to all men.
The Lord is near.
6Be anxious for nothing, but in everything by prayer
and supplication with thanksgiving
let your requests be made known to God.

*7And the peace of God, which surpasses all
comprehension, will guard your hearts
and your minds in Christ Jesus."*

It was comforting to know that we didn't need to worry about anything, because the Lord was near; He was going with me through the process and giving me peace. So, as I continued the treatments, I had full assurance that everything was going to be fine.

It didn't take God long to confirm that promise from His Word. When Bobbie and I arrived at the clinic, I had to get my blood drawn, and then I had the radiation treatment. After treatment, I was scheduled to see both the radiologist and the oncologist. Both doctors were amazed at what they were seeing. The oncologist was surprised I wasn't showing any side effects, because I had received a heavy dose of chemo. Also, when the bloodwork came back, it was normal! God is good! I wasn't alone; as I was walking through this, He was walking with me.

As is typical of most long journeys, the remaining part of our journey was riddled with peaks and valleys, highs and lows. I admit that I didn't make it through this portion of the journey without some setbacks, but even with those hurdles, Bobbie and I knew God was with us, and I **never lost my sense of humor.**

"Always laugh when you can. It is cheap medicine."
– Lord Byron

Chapter 3
Fuel for the Journey

"A cheerful disposition is good for your health; gloom and doom leave you bone-tired."
– Proverbs 17:22 MSG

"If people only knew the healing power of laughter and joy, many of our fine doctors would be out of business."
– Catherine Ponder

Laughter is a Good Medicine

Scientists and doctors are beginning to confirm what the Bible says about joy and laughter—it does good like a medicine.

"A merry heart does good, like medicine,
But a broken spirit dries the bones."
– Proverbs 17:22

Norman Cousins was a perfect example of this principal. In 1964, Cousins, who was editor of the *Saturday Review,* took a trip to cold-war Russia. Being under any socialist or communist system, where an individual's movements can be monitored by the government, can potentially be very stressful; that is what Cousins experienced. Due to tight scheduling and miscommunication, he felt that his immune system became weakened, and susceptible to the diesel fumes from the nonstop construction around his hotel.

After returning to the United States, he was admitted to a hospital with severe pain, high fever, and near paralysis of the legs, neck and back. He was diagnosed with a life-threatening disease of the connective tissue called degenerative collagen illness. His doctor informed him only one in five-hundred survived and that he would die within a few months.

He disagreed and reasoned that if stress had somehow contributed to his illness (he was not sick before his trip to Russia) then positive emotions should help him feel better. With his doctors' consent, he checked himself out of the hospital and into a hotel across the street and began taking extremely high doses of vitamin C, while also exposing himself to a continuous stream of humorous films and similar "laughing matter." He later claimed that ten minutes of belly-rippling laughter would give him two hours of pain-free sleep, when nothing else—not even morphine—could help him.

His condition steadily improved, and he slowly regained use of his limbs. Within six months, he was back on his feet, and within two years he was able to return to his full-time job at the *Saturday Review*. His story baffled the scientific community and inspired a number of research projects.[1]

Norman Cousins was one of the most influential people in the field of laughter therapy. He used his notoriety as a writer, professor, and political activist to draw attention to a subject that may have otherwise remained in its infancy. In our own research, his case was the most cited, and for good reason; his condition was rapidly decreasing, and his own willpower saved him. He was living proof that laughter and positive thinking could save us from the most dire of circumstances. There have been many studies conducted that support the use of humor therapy, such as those by doctors Miller, Berk, Hayashi, and Jiang. Hopefully, as technology continues to increase, so will our understanding of how laughter affects our mental and physical health.[2]

Cousins wrote: "The human body experiences a powerful gravitational pull in the direction of hope.

---

[1] https://sites.google.com/site/laughofflife/page-1
[2] https://sites.google.com/site/laughofflife/page-7

That is why the patient's hopes are the physician's secret weapon. They are the hidden ingredients in any prescription."[3]

THE PRESCRIPTION THAT I DECIDED TO
TAKE WAS THE "GOS-PILLS."

*"Now faith is the substance of things hoped for,
the evidence of things not seen."*
– Hebrews 11:1

A Sense of Humor and Walking Through

Because I had my faith and hope in Jesus and His Word, I knew everything was going to be fine, so I determined that I wasn't going to let the original diagnosis get me down. I've always had a sense of humor, and I told Bobbie, "If I have to go through this, I might as well have fun." Even though at times it was hard and not always fun, I kept my sense of humor through it all.

Here is one ne example of keeping a sense of humor: Every time I was scheduled to see the radiologist, one of her nurses would weigh me. Because I have a youthful, mischievous side, when I would check in at the desk for my appointment, I would ask the receptionist if I could go back and weigh. When one of the nurses

---

[3] Norman Cousins Quotes. BrainyQuote.com, Xplore Inc,2018. https://www.brainyquote.com/quotes/norman_cousins_133088, accessed September 18, 2018.

would then take me back to record my weight, I (already knowing what I weighed) would put my hand on my forehead like I was concentrating. Then I would "guess" my weight to the exact ounce. Those nurses would look at me in amazement and I would act like it was no big deal. I was just that good!

Since I was having radiation treatments to my head and neck, before I could start treatment, I had to have a mesh mask form-fitted to my head. This is one of the reasons the doctor didn't want me to lose any weight. She wanted the mask to stay tightly fit to my head, so it wouldn't move during radiation. The radiation technician would lay me on the table of the radiation machine, clamp the mask to the table so I couldn't move, then she would use lasers to align where she needed to radiate. With the mesh mask and the red and green laser lights, it looked like something out of a mad scientist movie.

We asked the technician if Bobbie could take the grandkids back to watch the alignment, so they would better understand what was going on with their Papa. After all, they had been praying for me. They were excited to see the red and green lasers.

I also wanted Bobbie to take some pictures, so we could post them on our Facebook page. The technician agreed. After we posted the pictures, I asked the people who were following us on Facebook to give me a superhero name. One person suggested, *"The Man in the*

Iron Mask." A couple of people thought, *"Meshman,"* would be good. My son, Chris, said I looked like the villain from the new Batman movie. A good friend thought I should be called, *"Super Human,"* but I'm not; I'm just a man who, with God's help, was making the best of the situation, with humor.

> "If Satan can't steal your joy,
> he can't keep your goods."
> – Jerry Savelle

Mr. Clean is Alive and Well!

As I mentioned before, I had decided to go for the Mr. Clean look. Since I would be losing my hair, I wanted an earring to complete the look. One day our good friend, Cheryl, called and said she had an earring for me. She gave one earring to me and the other to her husband, Brian. He actually wore it to demonstrate his solidarity with me. It meant so much to have support from our good friends. I would wear that earring every time I was scheduled for a treatment at the treatment center. People would smile when they saw me and my earring; they could see that there was something different about us. We were not full of gloom and despair. This gave us opportunities to share Jesus with others and share that He was our hope and our strength.

> *"...Do not sorrow, for the*
> *joy of the Lord is your strength."*
> – Nehemiah 8:10

One day, I showed up at the treatment center without my earring, and everyone wanted to know what was wrong. They asked me why I wasn't wearing my earring. That was when I realized how much joy and hope wearing that earring brought to others. I asked Bobbie to carry it in her purse, so it was always available. From then on, no matter how badly I felt, I would wear that earring.

> *"This is the day the LORD has made;*
> *We will rejoice and be glad in it."*
> – Psalm 118:24

During the journey, I decided I wanted some special shirts made to wear while walking through to my victory. Bobbie and I talked to some friends of ours, Mark and Stacie Morris, who owned a screen print shop, and I explained to them what I was envisioning. I wanted a shirt designed with a picture of Mr. Clean wearing his earring. Mark and Stacie created a t-shirt that said, *Michael "Mr. Clean" Baker*. When I wore my earring with my specially designed shirt, there actually *was* some resemblance between Mr. Clean and me!

The next shirt Mark and Staci created for me had a picture of actor Telly Salvalas as Kojak, with his signature Tootsie-Roll Pop. The shirt, along with the image, also featured Kojak's famous saying, "Who loves ya, baby?"

Based on the hit song from the early 90's, *"I'm Too Sexy,"* by Right Said Fred, the last shirt said, *"I'm too sexy for my hair."*

In addition to my Mr. Clean look, these shirts brought joy and hope to others we encountered during the course of my treatment. I believe because other patients watched me going through the same thing they were experiencing, yet doing so with joy and hope, it was an encouragement to them that they, too, could make it through.

> "Against the assault of laughter,
> nothing can stand."
> – Mark Twain

Several weeks into the treatment, my throat was so sore I couldn't talk. One day, Bobbie and I were in our living room, and I needed to tell her something. Adding humor to the situation, I picked up my phone, and I texted her. When her phone went off, she looked up and saw it was me, then turned to me and smiled. I had heard of young people communicating this way, but I never thought I would be one of them!

The Witness of an Earring

Another humorous moment during our journey occurred with our friends, Brian and Cheryl. One Saturday night, about six weeks after I finished my last treatment, Bobbie received a call from Cheryl. She was the leader over the women's ministry at our church, and Bobbie was her assistant. She wanted Bobbie to go with her and her husband, Brian, to downtown Tulsa to find a place in advance for fifty ladies to have coffee after a Beth Moore women's meeting.

Bobbie asked me if I wanted to go with them. It was the first day that I felt up to getting out, so I said, "Yes," even though I didn't have much strength or look good. My neck and face were still burnt from the radiation. By this time, I had lost several pounds, and my clothes were a little baggy. I looked like I was dying of AIDS (God can heal AIDS, too)!

As Bobbie and I were heading downtown to meet up with Cheryl and Brian, we received a call from Cheryl. She wanted to know if I had my earring with me. Of course, Bobbie had it in her purse. Cheryl said Brian was wearing his and wanted me to wear mine.

Brian was a math teacher at a local college, and he looked the part—very distinguished with grey hair. His earring did *not* match his look. My earring, on the other hand, matched my appearance well.

We met up and started walking around downtown. Picture this: I looked like I was a dying man walking around with my lovely wife, and Brian looked very distinguished walking around with his lovely wife, yet both of us wearing an earring. It was a real contradiction!

As we strolled from place to place, walking around slowly because of my lack of energy, people would just stop and stare at us. They were either too afraid, or embarrassed, to talk to us and find out what was actually going on. When we entered the Topeca Coffee shop, I was tired, so I told Bobbie, Cheryl, and Brian I was going to sit at one of the tables with soft chairs. As I sat and waited for them to order, I noticed a young man and two young ladies at another table staring at me.

After Bobbie, Cheryl, and Brian sat down, the young man came over and said, "My friends told me not to come over because you might beat me up, but I just have to ask: What is going on with the earrings?" I thought that was funny, because I didn't look like I was in any shape to beat up anyone! So, I looked at everyone and said, "I've got this."

I went on to explain that I had just finished treatment for stage four cancer, that Brian was my friend and wore the earring to show his solidarity with me. I was also able to share Jesus with him and explain how He had been with me every step of the way.

Just as I didn't lose my sense of humor and let the circumstances get me down, you don't have to allow the circumstances of your life get you down either.

"The most wasted of all days
is one without laughter."
– E. E. Cummings

Chapter 4
Grace for the Journey

"One of the primary hindrances
to people receiving from the Lord
is they know more about their problem,
sickness, and disease than they
know about the remedy:
God's Word and the
finished work of the cross!"
– Greg Mohr

"It is in our darkest
moments that we must
focus to see the light."
– Aristotle

Go to God's Word

Where is the first place people go when they have a medical problem? The internet? Family and friends? That's where most people go. They want to learn all they can about the problem instead of getting the answer to the problem. The answer to sickness and disease is the Word of God.

The Word of God will be the light in your darkest moment.

"Your word is a lamp to my feet
And a light to my path."
– Psalm 119:105

"My child, pay attention to what I say.
Listen carefully to my words.
21Don't lose sight of them.
Let them penetrate deep into your heart,
22for they bring life to those who find them,
and healing to their whole body.
23Guard your heart above all else,
for it determines the course of your life."
– Proverbs 4:20-23 NLT

When the scripture says, *"Listen carefully to my words,"* it is talking about the Word of God. When you meditate on the Word, and get it deep inside you, it will bring life and health to your whole body. When you believe God's Word for healing, it produces life and wholeness.

Here are some promises from God that encouraged our faith during our journey:

"...for I am watching over
my word to perform it."
– Jeremiah 1:12 ESV

"So, shall my word be that
goes forth from My mouth;
It shall not return to Me void,
But it shall accomplish what I please,
And it shall prosper in the thing
for which I sent it."
– Isaiah 55:11

This is good news. As you read the following healing scriptures and believe what they say, you can have confidence they are true and will come to pass, because God is watching over His Word, and it will accomplish what He said it would.

Here is what God's Word says about healing:

"He sent His word and healed them,
And delivered them from their destructions."
– Psalm 107:20

God gave us His Word so we would know about healing. We don't need to go to friends, family or the internet for answers. All the answers we need are in God's Word.

Jesus Purchased Our Healing

"But He was wounded for our transgressions,
He was bruised for our iniquities;
The chastisement for our peace was upon Him,
And by His stripes we are healed."
– Isaiah 53:5

"Who Himself bore our sins
in His own body on the tree,
that we, having died to sins,
might live for righteousness—
by whose stripes you were healed."
– 1 Peter 2:24

Jesus purchased our healing when He was beaten and hung on the Cross.

"Christ has redeemed us from the curse of the law,
having become a curse for us (for it is written,
'Cursed is everyone who hangs on a tree')."
– Galatians 3:13

Because He purchased our healing, all we have to do is believe and receive it. For the Bible declares,

"For assuredly, I say to you, whoever says to
this mountain, 'Be removed and be cast into
the sea,' and does not doubt in his heart, but
believes that those things he says will be done,
he will have whatever he says.

*24Therefore, I say to you, whatever things you
ask when you pray, believe that you receive them,
and you will have them."*
– Mark 11:23-24

Speak God's Word

Cancer may seem like an insurmountable mountain, but all you need to do is speak to it, in Jesus' Name, and believe God's Word is true, and sickness must leave your body.

*"Beloved, I wish above all things that thou mayest
prosper and be in health, even as thy soul prospereth."*
– 3 John 2 KJV

Notice, God says that *above all things* He wants you to prosper **and be in health** as your soul prospers. God doesn't want you sick, He wants you well. Again, **God gets glory when you're well, not when you're sick**.

*"The thief does not come except to steal,
and to kill, and to destroy.
I have come that they may have life,
and that they may have it more abundantly."*
– John 10:10

You can't have the kind of abundant life God wants you to have when you're sick. Here are some "Gos-pills" you can take to have that abundant life. You can take these as many times a day as you want without any adverse side effects! Read all these scriptures daily, and let them get deep into your heart. As you do, the healing power of God will begin to manifest in you.

"Many are the afflictions of the righteous,
But the Lord delivers him out of them all."
– Psalm 34:19

"'For I will restore health to you,
And heal you of your wounds,' says the LORD..."
– Jeremiah 30:17

"O Lord my God, I cried out to You,
And You healed me."
– Psalm 30:2

"Heal me, O LORD, and I shall be healed;
Save me, and I shall be saved, For You are my
praise."
– Jeremiah 17:14

"Bless the LORD, O my soul;
And all that is within me, bless His holy name!
2Bless the LORD, O my soul,
And forget not all His benefits:
3Who forgives all your iniquities,
Who heals all your diseases."
– Psalm 103:1-3

God heals **all** our diseases! This includes cancer. So, you could say it this way: *Who heals all my cancer.*

*"How God anointed Jesus of Nazareth with the Holy
Spirit and with power, who went about doing good
and healing all who were oppressed by the devil, for
God was with Him."*
– Acts 10:38

Notice, Jesus went about doing good and healing
all. He did not go around making people sick.

Redeemed from the Curse

*"Christ has redeemed us from the curse of the law,
having become a curse for us
(for it is written, 'Cursed is everyone
who hangs on a tree').*"
– Galatians 3:13

Cancer is a curse from which we have been redeemed.

*"Jesus Christ is the same
yesterday, today, and forever."*
– Hebrews 13:8

This means that the healings Jesus did in the past,
He is still doing today!

*"...he cast out the spirits with a word
and healed all who were sick.
17This was to fulfill*

what was spoken by the prophet Isaiah:
'He took our illnesses and bore our diseases.'"
— Matthew 8:16-17

"Death and life are in the power of the tongue,
And those who love it will eat its fruit."
— Proverbs 18:21

Since death and life are in the power of the tongue, instead of speaking death over yourself, begin to speak life.

Confessions for Your Healing

Here are some confessions[4] based upon God's Word to speak over yourself as many times a day as you need. As you read these out loud, let them permeate your whole body.

I am healed. I will live and not die. I will fulfill my destiny. I will fulfill my calling. I will live out my days, in Jesus' Name!

My faith in God is strong. I pay no attention to my body. I am healed. I will live a good life.

I am motivated and strong. I hear the voice of God, and I obey His commands. My

---

[4] www.HopeFaithPrayer.com

faith is alive, working, and strong. My faith is growing faster than the cancer.

I curse the cancer cells, and they are dying, in Jesus' Name. The cancer cells are dying, and my cells are being renewed every day.

Lord, I hear Your voice. I have the faith to win this battle. I will win. I will overcome through faith in God. I have the victory. The treatments and medications are working, and I will not have any side effects.

God's mercy and grace are sufficient for me. His power is burning out the cancer in my body. His mercy overshadows all that I am and all that I do. Lord, I receive Your mercy. I receive Your healing for me.

My hope is in God and in His promises alone. I will be healed. I will be whole. God is big enough. God is faithful enough.

Jesus paid the price for my healing on the Cross, and I will receive it, Jesus, and I will not have this healing stolen from us.

I curse this sickness, and I curse its effects. I will be made whole. I will not suffer long-term damage. I will not suffer side effects from the treatments. I refuse this sickness in my body, and I curse it, in Jesus' Name. It will come to an end.

I will be healed from this cancer. I will be cancer-free, in Jesus' Name! I am going to live and not die. The power of God is real. It is working in my body. It is healing me. It is restoring me. The Spirit of God is killing the cancer cells. My body's cells are strong and alive. I am alive and well. I am healthy and whole.

It does not matter what I feel like. It does not matter what my mind thinks. My heart knows that I am whole. My heart knows that I am healed, in Jesus' Name.

God is alive. God is real. His Word is real. His Word is healing me. His Word will do it. I am healed, in Jesus' Name!

As you daily dwell on God's promises to you, and hide them in your heart, always remember:

> *"...Not one word has failed*
> *of all his good promise..."*
> – 1 Kings 8:56

Chapter 5
The Final Stage of the Journey

"To get through the hardest journey we need take only
one step at a time, but we must keep on stepping."
– Chinese Proverb

Our Thousand-Mile Journey

Even though August 19th was my last chemo
treatment and August 27th was my last radiation
treatment, our *thousand-mile journey* was far from
over. The chemo and radiation would continue to
work for at least three more weeks, and the journey
would have its ups and downs. I would have good
days and rough days. We knew that through it all,

God was with us, and all we had to do was keep on stepping to finish our healing journey.

"So, let's not get tired of doing what is good.
At just the right time we will reap a harvest of
blessing if we don't give up."
– Galatians 6:9 NLT

As we were coming to the end of the treatment phase of the journey, we ran into some complications. My cells were not absorbing fluid, and I was becoming dehydrated. I had to go in and have IV fluids two to three times a week. I was also in a lot of pain from the radiation burns on my neck. Bobbie would have to give me pain medication every few hours.

In addition, she was taking me to all my treatments and to receive IV fluids. As a result, she was getting very little sleep and was becoming physically exhausted. Because she is such a loving person, she was more concerned about me than she was about herself.

Here is a post that she wrote the day after my last radiation treatment:

Ok, it's a new day! I asked the Lord this morning for strength, because I am tired. As I walked into the treatment room for Michael to get IV fluids, a nurse who is a believer in Jesus came up to me and said, "The Lord spoke something to me this morning in my prayer time. He said, 'The Holy Spirit gives us strength.'" I received it from God. He is the One who energizes us and gives us help.

> "... 'My grace is sufficient for you, for My strength is made perfect in weakness.'..."
> – 2 Corinthians 12:9

Thank You, Father, for sending us the Holy Spirit. Sometimes I think I take Him for granted. Today is a new day and I being fully aware of that:

> "I can do all things through Christ who strengthens me!"
> – Philippians 4:13

Blessings and Love. I have been giving Michael pain meds every four hours now, but they aren't working much. The doctor changed it today to something stronger! Praise!

This is one example of how Bobbie was more concerned about me than herself. She knew that after my last chemo treatment I would be in the *nadir phase*, which means for three weeks my blood levels would go down, my immune system would be weakened, and then the healing would begin.

She also knew that meant that for the next three weeks, she would be taking care of me night and day and would get very little rest. Even more, she knew that with the Word of the Lord, "The Holy Spirit gives us strength," He was going to give her the strength she needed.

Here is another example of her unselfish love for me:

Good evening prayer partners. Today is a rough day. Michael's blood work is really low, as he is still in the nadir phase. It's uphill from here. He received fluids today and usually gets a boost from it. Our anniversary was Saturday the 31st, and we were unable to celebrate, but we will soon be able to do something very special! We are thankful for LIFE!

This was posted on her birthday. Not only did she not get to celebrate our anniversary, she didn't get to celebrate her birthday, yet she was still finding things to be thankful for.

Just three days after my final radiation treatment, I went in for some blood work. When we got the results, they were all normal. We were praising God for this. So, on Sunday, I decided to go to church. Afterwards, I went home, took a nap, and then went to my brother's birthday party. We didn't stay long because I was still weak, but at least I was able to go. The next day, I had to go into the treatment center to receive more fluids. Usually, after I'd had some IV fluids, I would feel better and try to do more than I should. This is the reason my journey was up and down.

Monday, September 9th

On September 9th, thirteen days out from my last radiation:

Good morning to our wonderful friends and family! What would we ever do without Jesus? He is Wonderful, Counselor, Almighty God, Prince of Peace, the Great Physician! Michael is doing so well. He (Michael) drove me to church and home yesterday. He helped with the New Members class that we oversee and sat through the whole church service. He is getting stronger every day. He does have a low-grade temperature this morning though. Praying it goes back to normal where it belongs. Today we go back for fluids.

Wednesday, September 11th

Two days later, on September 11th, fifteen days from my last radiation treatment, Bobbie posted this:

Good morning people of prayer! Together, through prayer and the power of God, we are seeing results. Michael went to work this morning for a few hours and drove himself. He is staying up more of the day. His color is back to normal and God is doing a quick healing! PRAISE! He does go back for fluids again tomorrow. I am leaving for Joyce Meyers' Women's convention in St. Louis early tomorrow. I'm leaving Chris in total charge for 3 days. He is such a blessing, and I know they will have a good Dad/son time building memories. Michael is progressing in the healing process so well, it's really something special to watch daily. Blessings to you all!

Monday, September 16th

On September 16th, Bobbie posted this:

Good evening to all of you! Michael is getting better every day. He hasn't had to have fluids since last Thursday. He is still a little weak, but it's amazing how well he is doing. We are so very thankful to our Father God and for all of you. I think he and Chris had a good time together. I had a wonderful time at Joyce Meyers' Women's Convention with two girlfriends. It was amazing and very encouraging to know how much God loves us, and how much He has for each one of us. Blessings to each one of you!!!!

Thursday, September 19th

The ups and downs continued. We thought I was healing nicely until three days later. On September 19th Bobbie posted this:

Yesterday was a hard day. Obviously, Michael needed fluids. He was weak and dizzy, and his eyes were sunken. We got him in around 11:30 and by 3:30, we were returning home. He really didn't feel himself until this morning. I'm not sure how long he will have to have IV fluids. We are four weeks out from chemo and I think his body should be back to normal. We are believing God for a quick recovery from this and speaking healing and health to his body, in Jesus' mighty Name. Thank you so much for your prayers.

Thursday, September 25th

One week later, just like a roller coaster, I was back up again, doing better.

Michael is doing well. He had IV fluids yesterday; he also had frozen yogurt for the first time. "First bite tasted good, no taste after that." He also drank chicken bouillon, and that also tasted good! Healing fast. Praise Father God! We are very thankful! God bless each one of you. Thank you for your love and support!

Tuesday, October 1st

October 1st, five weeks out as I steadily improved, this happened:

Good Morning! Michael is doing so well. His throat still hurts, and it's painful to eat and swallow, so we are holding off of it for a time. His strength is returning slowly. He is working half days this week. He is taking his formula and Gatorade with him. He is still needing pain meds twice a day to keep comfortable. Blessings to each of you. Thank you for standing with us in prayer through this.

Sunday, October 6th

And healing continued. On October 6th, this was posted:

Good Evening! It's a great day to be alive. Jesus is truly the Healer! Michael is eating rice and soups and drinking water and Gatorade. Minimal pain to his throat now. He's getting stronger and stronger every day. He still needs to take a nap every day, but it's awesome to see the healing manifesting. Thanks so much for standing with us through this. We pray Father bless each one of you in a special way so that you would just know it was His hand that did it. We love you all!!!!

Thursday, October 10th

Good afternoon, beloved friends and prayer warriors. Again, I would like to thank you for your prayers and words of encouragement. As Bobbie has posted, I'm working half days. It is so good to work and be productive. I have a couple of prayer requests. First, continue to pray for my salivary glands, as my mouth is still really dry. Also, for the continued healing of my throat. Even though my throat does not hurt, I'm still having some difficulty swallowing. Also, pray that my taste buds are completely healed. Lastly, please pray for my hearing. I'm having trouble hearing high pitched sounds. We feel so blessed that each one of you are following our journey. We thank God for each one of you. Mike N Bobbie.

Thursday, October 24th

Sometimes miracles happen, and we don't even recognize it. On October 24th this was posted:

Hi to all of our friends and family, we know you are wondering how Michael is doing. He is really doing well. His color is back, strength is returning rapidly, he is able to eat soft food meals now and is decreasing his G-tube feedings. His voice is still a little raspy, but he can talk well. His taste buds are back; he can actually taste food. Praise! He is approximately 6 weeks out from the last radiation and 7 weeks out from chemo, and this is really a miracle. He spoke to a client the other day who told him of a friend that had the same treatment 1½ years ago and Michael's voice is better than his. Praise! We are so very grateful for Jesus walking through this with us and for all of you standing with us in prayer. This truly is to the glory of God!!!!!! Blessings and Love – Bobbie and Michael.

Tuesday, October 29th

Good Morning. I know you all want us to update you every so often. Michael is continuing to get stronger. Last weekend was very busy with fellowships, friends, birthday party, and grandchildren, and it really wore him out. He didn't get his nap on Saturday or Sunday, and it took a toll on him. He's realizing he has to pace himself. He has backed off of eating, realizing he was trying to push himself too quickly. Thank you for your continued prayers. One thing we would specifically like you to believe God with us for: After radiation to the head and neck, there is always potential for damage to the jaw bones, which wouldn't be pretty. Continue to pray for restoration to all of his bones in his face and neck. God is good and His supernatural far exceeds the natural.

"...all things are possible to him who believes."
– Mark 9:23

Blessings and Love, Bobbie.

Tuesday, December 3rd

December 3rd, fourteen weeks out from my last treatment, and I was back to work fulltime:

Good afternoon, beloved prayer warriors. I know it has been 5 weeks since our last post and I apologize for that. There has not been a lot to report (which is not a bad thing). Bobbie and I just returned from our annual Thanksgiving trip to Nebraska to be with her family. As always, we had a good visit.

Yesterday, I started back to work fulltime. I was pretty tired when I got home at 5:30, but I made it. Because I was so tired I went to bed by 8:30. The good news is that I'm getting my strength back. Also, I'm eating more every day. I have cut back on my tube feedings to 3 a day. I feel like I'm doing so good that when I finish the remaining formula next Friday I will stop the tube feedings, altogether. I'm hoping to have the tube taken out by the end of the year. Now for the news I've been waiting on. They finally called to schedule a PET scan for Thursday the 5th. Then on Wednesday the 11th I see the ENT doctor, and on Thursday the 12th, I see the radiologist and the oncologist to go over the scan.

So, after my visit on the 12th, we should get the good report that the cancer is all gone. Thank you all for your prayers and support through this journey. Because of the blessings of God and your prayers and support, this journey will be successful.

We love each of you. Mike N Bobbie.

Thursday, December 12th

December 12th: And the miracle healing continues.

Hi to all our friends and family! Michael received a clean bill of health today! The PET scan was normal, the blood work was totally normal, including the thyroid. THAT IS A MIRACLE!

Thanks so much for standing with us in prayer through this journey! DOCTORS TREAT, BUT JESUS HEALS. They will be scheduling outpatient surgery for the port and G-tube removal. Hopefully, this will happen before the new year, since we have paid our deductible through December.

Blessings and Love, Michael and Bobbie

Friday, December 27th

Good morning, beloved friends and family. As the busy Christmas season comes to an end, I want to take a few moments and reflect on what the birth of Jesus means. Not only did He come as Savior, He came as Healer. Bobbie and I are praising God for the healing that I have received. I'm like the one leper in Luke 17 who came and fell at Jesus' feet, thanking Him for the healing. Jesus asked, "Were there not 10 healed? Where are the other 9?" Well, I'm shouting it from the rooftop: JESUS HEALED ME!

Now for more praise reports. We posted last time that we would like my G-tube and port taken out by the end of the year. Well, I went to see the surgeon on Monday, and he took my G-tube out right in his office. Then he asked me when I wanted the port out. Of course, I said by the end of the year. So, he is going to take it out on New Year's Eve! We are praising God for this. We would like to thank each one of you who have faithfully followed us and prayed for us. We hope these posts have blessed you. We will continue to post every couple of weeks for those who want to continue to follow "The Journey." We love you all! Mike N Bobbie.

Tuesday, January 28th, 2014

Good morning, beloved. Thank you so much for your faithfulness. Just a quick update on my progress.

I'm just now fully recovering from my surgery to remove the port. There were no real complications, only stiffness in my left arm. My muscles were knotted up because I was favoring the port site. They are finally relaxing, and the pain is almost all gone. As far as my strength goes, I'm about 90%. My salivary gland is about 75%. Because of this, I'm able to teach Sunday School. Praise God! I'm able to teach! What the devil meant for bad (trying to take away my voice) Jesus turned for my good and His glory. Yours in Christ. Michael N Bobbie.

Wednesday, February 12th

Good morning! Blessings. After my last post, I was asked how my hearing was doing. Unfortunately, it has not gotten any better. Also, my arm is still hurting. I think it might be a pinched nerve. If it does not get any better, I will have it checked out on my next doctor's visit. Now I would like to share this with you: A couple of weeks ago at church, a friend came up to me and said, "Michael you look so good, you don't even look like you had cancer." And I said to her "Isn't that just like Jesus to not only heal you of cancer, but make it look like you never even had it?" Still praising Jesus! Michael N Bobbie

Thursday, March 27th

On March 3rd, I had a PET scan, and went to see the ear, nose and throat doctor. The reason for the

PET scan was that when I had the last one in December, they saw 2 swollen lymph nodes in my stomach. One was small, and one was medium. When they did the scan on March 3rd, the cancer on the base of my tongue was gone, but the lymph nodes were still there and still the same size.

When I saw Dr. Atul, the ENT, he scoped my throat. That is where they put a small camera through my nose and down my throat. He said my throat and tongue were clear. PRAISE GOD!

Another confirmation that the cancer is gone: On March 13th I went and had my teeth cleaned. One of the side effects of the radiation they said is that my teeth would deteriorate. When she cleaned my teeth, she was amazed. She said they were in the best shape they have ever been. Another PRAISE GOD!

On March 17th, I went to see Mackie Sutton, who is the PA for my oncologist. This was for what they call a cancer survivor briefing. Even though she was not the one who ordered the PET scan, we talked about it. I told her God did not heal me of throat cancer just so I would get lymphoma. She agreed and said "people of faith" have a higher survival rate than those who don't have faith. Of course, we knew that, but it's nice to have a medical professional confirm that.

On March 18th, we saw the radiologist. She is the one who ordered the PET scan. She said she wanted to keep an eye on the swollen lymph nodes, so she wants me to have another scan at the end of May. Like I said, *God did not heal me of cancer so I can get lymphoma.* The Devil is a liar.

We sang the song "In Jesus' Name" at church a couple of weeks ago. It is the same song I listened to over and over through the cancer treatments. I know it was God saying it will be all right.

Here is the song:

> God is fighting for us / God is on our side
> He has overcome / Yes, He has overcome
> We will not be shaken / We will not be moved
> Jesus You are here
>
> Carrying our burdens / Covering our shame
> He has overcome / Yes, He has overcome
> We will not be shaken / We will not be moved
> Jesus you are here
>
> I will live / I will not die
> The resurrection power of Christ
> Alive in me and I am free
> In Jesus' Name
> I will live / I will not die
> I will declare and lift You high
> Christ revealed / And I am healed
> In Jesus' Name
>
> God is fighting for us / Pushing back the darkness
> Lighting up the Kingdom / That cannot be shaken
> In the Name of Jesus / Enemy's defeated
> And we will shout it out / Shout it out[5]

Monday, June 9th

Good morning faithful ones and prayer warriors. I had another PET scan on May 29th. On Thursday, June 5th, I went to see Dr. Cole, the oncologist, and Dr. Nguyen, the radiologist, to get the results of the scan. I saw Dr. Cole first. Before I saw Dr. Cole they weighed me. I weighed 203 lbs. Since the end of treatment, I have lost 34 lbs. Hopefully, I will post a picture soon. He said the cancer was gone in my throat. Praise God!

However, he said the four spots on my abdomen were still there. Three of them were the same size and one had gotten a little bigger. He suggested that I have them biopsied, but that would mean surgery. I said, "No" to the surgery. I told him God did not heal me of cancer so I would get lymphoma. The devil is a liar.

He wanted to schedule a consultation with the surgeon, and I said that was fine. He also went over my blood work, which was the best it had been since treatment began. Another Praise God!

Next, we went downstairs to see Dr. Nguyen. Before she came to see me, we were informed she went upstairs to consult with Dr. Cole. When she came in, she basically said the same thing, that she wanted me to have the spots biopsied, because she did not know what they were. She said it could be inflammation, or it could be lymphoma, but wasn't sure because

I wasn't showing any symptoms of lymphoma. Again, I said that God did not heal me of cancer so I would come down with lymphoma. The devil is a liar.

She then scoped me. She said it looked good. She was going to schedule another scan around the first of December. Again, thank you for all of your love and prayers. Michael.

Wednesday, August 27th

Good afternoon, beloved friends and prayer warriors. Today is the first-year anniversary of my last radiation treatment. Praise God! This past year has been a challenge, but because of the goodness of God and all of your love, prayers and support, Bobbie and I have overcome. I'm feeling good and getting back to normal. My stamina is still not what it used to be. I feel like I'm about 80%.

On my last post on June 9th, I said I weighed 203 lbs. Today I weighed 199 lbs. so I'm maintaining my weight. Praise God. (That also means that since I first went to see my PCP back on April 25th of 2013 that I've lost 63 lbs. I would not recommend this "diet" to anyone.)

My taste is coming back. I'm able to swallow most things. The heat here in Oklahoma is taking a bigger toll on me than normal, but I'm going to make it. I will make another post next week and fill you in on what God is doing in our lives. We love and appreciate each one of you.

Tuesday, September 2nd

Good afternoon, beloved friends and prayer warriors. First, we would like to thank each one of you for walking with us on this journey. It's been an amazing journey. As most of you know, I have a call of God on my life to do ministry; that is why the devil tried to take my voice. As you can see, he didn't succeed. Here I am teaching Sunday School. The Lord has healed my voice so that I can minister the Gospel.

So, now I would like to share what the Lord has in store for me and Bobbie. On Thursday, August 21st, the Lord spoke to me while I was on my way home from work. He said He wanted me to go to Andrew Wommack's Charis Bible College, in Colorado Springs. I said to the Lord that He would have to tell Bobbie, because it would be hard for her to leave the grandkids. At 2:00 that same day, the Lord told Bobbie that we would be moving to Colorado.

So, when I got home she said to sit down, because she had something to tell me. After she told me, we started making plans to move. When God tells us to do something, we immediately obey. On Saturday the 23rd, I told my "spiritual mom," that we were going to sell the house. She called some mutual friends to tell them, and they said they wanted to buy our house because they had always liked it.

On Monday the 25th, they told us they were interested in our house. On Friday the 29th, they got preapproved. So, God sold our house in about a week, without us even putting it on the market. Praise God! So, as this journey is coming to a close, another journey is about to begin. So, we still covet your prayers, love and support. The new *Michael and Bobbie's Journey* begins with a single step of faith...

"But without faith it is impossible to please Him, for he who comes to God must believe that He is, and that He is a rewarder of those who diligently seek Him."
– Hebrews 11:6

Chapter 6
You're Not Alone on the Journey

"...He Himself has said,
'I will never leave you nor forsake you.'"
– Hebrews 13:5

"Good company in a journey
makes the way seem shorter."
– Izaak Walton

Heading in the Same Direction

I know when I'm on a journey, it's so much more enjoyable when I have Bobbie along to navigate. And this has certainly been a journey I'm so thankful I had her along.

We knew the Word of God said:

> *"Can two people walk together*
> *without agreeing on the direction?"*
> – Amos 3:3 NLT

We were heading in the same direction, toward my complete and total healing. She was there to help, comfort, and most importantly, pray with me. When we prayed, we were in agreement with one another, believing the Word of God, knowing that Jesus said:

> *"Again I say to you that if two*
> *of you agree on earth concerning*
> *anything that they ask,*
> *it will be done for them*
> *by My Father in heaven."*
> – Matthew 18:19

As you are taking this journey with us, you might be saying, "Michael, I'm glad you had Bobbie with you on this journey, but I have no one to walk with me." I want to encourage you that you are not alone. Jesus is, *"a friend who sticks closer than a brother"* (Proverbs 18:24).

Meredith Andrews wrote in her song, *"You're Not Alone"*:

> You're not alone
> for I am here
> Let me wipe away
> your every fear

My love, I've never
left your side
I have seen you through
the darkest night
And I'm the One
who's loved you all your life[6]

With or without a family, Jesus will be with you every step of your journey. As you are going through your darkest night, just know the Bible says:

"...'Fear not, for I have redeemed you;
I have called you by your name;
You are Mine.
[2]When you pass through the waters,
I will be with you; And through the rivers,
they shall not overflow you.
When you walk through the fire,
you shall not be burned,
Nor shall the flame scorch you.
[3]For I am the Lord your God...'"
– Isaiah 43:1-3

Also, be confident in this:

"The Lord is the one who goes ahead of you;
He will be with you.
He will not fail you or forsake you.
Do not fear or be dismayed."
– Deuteronomy 31:8 NASB

The Lord has already gone ahead of you, so you have nothing to fear.

"The Lord is my shepherd; I have all that I need.
2He lets me rest in green meadows;
he leads me beside peaceful streams.
3He renews my strength.
He guides me along right paths,
bringing honor to His name.
4Even when I walk through the darkest valley,
I will not be afraid, for you are close beside me.
Your rod and your staff protect and comfort me.
5You prepare a feast for me
in the presence of my enemies.
You honor me by anointing my head with oil.
My cup overflows with blessings.
6Surely your goodness and unfailing love
will pursue me
all the days of my life,
and I will live in the house of the LORD forever."
– Psalm 23 NLT

As you journey with Jesus, here is another thing He will do for you:

"He who dwells in the secret place of the Most High
Shall abide under the shadow of the Almighty.
2I will say of the LORD,
'He is my refuge and my
fortress; My God, in Him I will trust.'
3Surely He shall deliver you

from the snare of the fowler
And from the perilous pestilence.
4He shall cover you with His feathers,
And under His wings you shall take refuge;
His truth shall be your shield and buckler.
5You shall not be afraid of the terror by night,
Nor of the arrow that flies by day,
6Nor of the pestilence that walks in darkness,
Nor of the destruction that lays waste at noonday.
7A thousand may fall at your side,
And ten thousand at your right hand;
But it shall not come near you.
8Only with your eyes shall you look,
And see the reward of the wicked.
9Because you have made the LORD, who is my refuge,
Even the Most High, your dwelling place,
10No evil shall befall you,
Nor shall any plague come near your dwelling;
11For He shall give His angels charge over you,
To keep you in all your ways.
12In their hands they shall bear you up,
Lest you dash your foot against a stone.
13You shall tread upon the lion and the cobra,
The young lion and the serpent
you shall trample underfoot.
14'Because he has set his love upon Me,
therefore I will deliver him;
I will set him on high,
because he has known My name.
15He shall call upon Me,
and I will answer him;
I will be with him in trouble;

I will deliver him and honor him.
16With long life I will satisfy him,
And show him My salvation."
– Psalm 91

"'Tis so sweet to walk with Jesus,
Step by step and day by day;
Stepping in His very footprints,
Walking with Him all the way."
– Rev. A.B. Simpson

As I took this journey, I am so thankful that Bobbie was with me. However, I'm even more thankful that the Lord Jesus was journeying with me. I could not have made it through without Him. As you've taken this journey with us, we hope you've encountered the Lord Jesus Christ the Healer. He wants to walk with you because He loves you; all you have to do is come to Jesus and ask and believe that what you ask you shall receive.

Come to Me

Michael R. Baker

COME TO ME, SAYS THE LORD
COME TO ME
LET ME BE IN YOUR LIFE
ALL YOU NEED ME TO BE
I WILL HEAL ALL YOUR HURTS,
YOUR PAIN AND MISERY
IF YOU'LL JUST COME TO ME.

SEEK MY FACE, SAYS THE LORD
SEEK MY FACE
AND I WILL SHOW YOU MY MERCY,
MY LOVE AND MY GRACE
THERE IS NOT A SIN SO BAD
THAT MY BLOOD CANNOT ERASE
IF YOU WILL JUST SEEK MY FACE.

HEAR MY VOICE, SAYS THE LORD
HEAR MY VOICE
HE WHO HAS EARS TO HEAR
WILL MAKE THE RIGHT CHOICE
NO MATTER WHAT THE CIRCUMSTANCE
IN THE MIDST YOU CAN REJOICE
IF YOU WILL JUST HEAR MY VOICE.

CALL ON MY NAME, SAYS THE LORD
CALL ON MY NAME.
MY NAME IS JESUS
THE NAME ABOVE ALL NAMES
AND WHEN YOU DO
YOU WILL NEVER BE THE SAME
IF YOU WILL JUST CALL ON MY NAME.

COME TO ME, SAYS THE LORD
COME TO ME
I LOVE YOU SO MUCH
I DIED ON CALVARY'S TREE
SO WE COULD BE TOGETHER
FOR ALL ETERNITY
SO, JUST COME TO ME.

Chapter 7
Final Destination

"At any given moment you have the power to say,
'This is not how the story is going to end.'"
– Unknown

*"And what do you benefit if you gain the whole world
but lose your own soul?"*
– Mark 8:36 NLT

As we're coming to the end of this healing journey, you have the power to say how your journey will end. Is getting healed the final destination, or is there more to the journey? What would it benefit you if you got healed but lost your soul?

There is more to this journey, and I want to tell you how to take the first step on the *"eternal journey."*

There are a few things you need to know before you start this eternal journey. First, God wants to have a personal relationship with you. He wants you to live in Heaven with Him. The Bible states that eternal life is a free gift from God.

"For the wages of sin is death, but the gift of God is eternal life in Christ Jesus our Lord."
– Romans 6:23

Because eternal life is a free gift from God, we can't work for it, we can't earn it, and we don't deserve it. We can't be so good to cause God to love us more, and we can't be so bad to cause Him to love us less. God loves us because He *is* love.

This is how much God loves us:

"For God so loved the world that He gave His only begotten Son, that whoever believes in Him should not perish but have everlasting life. 17For God did not send His Son into the world to condemn the world, but that the world through Him might be saved."
– John 3:16-17

When did God show His love toward us?

"But God demonstrates His own love toward us, in that while we were still sinners, Christ died for us."
– Romans 5:8

Since no one can earn their way to Heaven, how do we get there? We all get there the same way: by the grace of God through faith in Jesus.

"For by grace you have been saved through faith,
and that not of yourselves; it is the gift of God,
9Not of works, lest anyone should boast."
– Ephesians 2:8-9

That's good news! However, here's some bad news: Not everyone gets into Heaven. The reason is sin. Sin is the roadblock that keeps people out of Heaven.

Simply stated, sin is not believing in or obeying God. The Bible says everyone has sinned, and God will hold us accountable.

"For all have sinned and
fall short of the glory of God."
– Romans 3:23

For us sinners, that is bad news. However, there is more good news. The Bible says that Jesus died on the Cross to forgive our sin. If sin can keep us out of Heaven, the only way we can get there is by having our sin forgiven.

The only way our sins can be forgiven is through Jesus, who died on the Cross to forgive our sins. If sin could have been forgiven any other way, the crucifixion would have been a waste of time. Christ died for our sins, was buried, and rose again on the third day, according to the Scriptures.

> *"For I delivered to you first of all that which*
> *I also received: that Christ died for our sins*
> *according to the Scriptures,*
> *4and that He was buried, and that*
> *He rose again the third day*
> *according to the Scriptures."*
> – 1 Corinthians 15:3-4

That's really good news!

If we want to go to Heaven and spend eternity with God, we must act on our belief in what Jesus did on the Cross. We must trust Christ. The way we trust Christ is by admitting that we are helpless apart from Him. Without faith in Jesus, we are all destined to spend eternity without Him. We admit our need for Christ by confessing that it was our sin that put Him on the Cross. Trusting Christ means accepting the responsibility for sin, and by faith, receiving the forgiveness of sins He offers.

> *"That if you confess with your mouth the Lord Jesus*
> *and believe in your heart that God raised Him from*
> *the dead, you will be saved. 10For with the heart one*
> *believes unto righteousness, and with the mouth*
> *confession is made unto salvation."*
> – Romans 10:9-10

About the Author

Michael and his wife Bobbie have spent the last thirty years serving the Body of Christ in the area of the Ministry of Helps, seventeen of which were at Grace Church in Tulsa, Oklahoma under the leadership of Pastor Bob Yandian. Michael is a 1985 graduate of Victory Bible Institute, Tulsa, Oklahoma, and a 2017 graduate of Charis Bible College Woodland Park, Colorado. He was an Associate Pastor of Living Stone Church in Coweta, Oklahoma for seven years.

Bobbie is a 2010 graduate of the Grace School of Ministry in Tulsa, Oklahoma, and also graduated Charis Bible College in 2017. Michael and Bobbie have a call to use their thirty years' experience to teach the Body of Christ in the area of Helps Ministry and to conduct marriage seminars to help strengthen marriages.

They currently reside in Woodland Park, Colorado where they serve as the Pastoral Care Pastors of River Rock Church in Colorado Springs for Pastor's Rick and Joann McFarland. They also teach a class at their Alma Mater, Charis Bible College, on Ministry of Helps titled *Developing a Heart of a Servant.*

Made in United States
Troutdale, OR
08/06/2023

CHOOSING TO RECEIVE JESUS CHRIST AS YOUR LORD AND SAVIOR IS THE MOST IMPORTANT DECISION YOU'LL EVER MAKE!

The best way I know for you to receive Christ as your Lord and Savior is to pray this simple prayer of faith:

"Jesus, I want to go to Heaven. I know I can't get to heaven because my sins are blocking the way. Forgive me of all my sins. I take personal responsibility for my sins by admitting them to you. I ask you to cleanse my heart, and make me a new person in You, right now.

I believe that You are the Son of God and that You died on the Cross for me. Jesus, I want to thank You for loving me enough to die for me. I accept all that Your shed blood bought for me on the Cross, and I receive you as my Savior and Lord. I'm turning my life over to you. Thank You for forgiving me. Help me to grow in my relationship with You.

In Your name I pray. Amen."

If you've just prayed this prayer, congratulations! You are a *new creature in Christ,* as the Bible declares:

> *"Therefore, if anyone is in Christ, he is a new creation; old things have passed away; behold, all things have become new."*
> – 2 Corinthians 5:17

Friend, you have a whole new journey with Jesus to look forward to, beginning this moment. Your slate is clean before God. Your spirit has been reborn because of Christ's great sacrifice and love for you.

If you prayed that prayer in faith, you are born again. Since you are born again, you believe God raises dead people, because, again, Romans 10:9-10 says, *"that if you confess with your mouth the Lord Jesus and believe in your heart that God has **RAISED HIM FROM THE DEAD**, you will be saved. [10]For with the heart one believes unto righteousness, and with the mouth confession is made unto salvation"* (emphasis mine).

> If God can raise dead people, then your
> problem is not too difficult for God.
> Whatever sickness you may have
> is not greater than death.
> Whatever financial problem you may have
> is not greater than death.
> Just as God conquered death,
> He can conquer your problem.
> – Paraphrased from Greg Mohr

"And if the Spirit of him who raised Jesus from the dead is living in you, he who raised Christ from the dead will also give life to your mortal bodies because of His Spirit who lives in you."
– Romans 8:11 NIV

Epilogue

As of this writing, it has been five years since my last radiation treatment and a lot has transpired. I have had two CAT scans, my throat scoped twice, and have been declared "cancer free." I knew I would be, because God did not heal me for the cancer to return.

In October 2014, fourteen months after my final radiation treatment, we started a new journey. We moved to Colorado to attend Charis Bible College, where we graduated from the third-year ministry school in 2017, with an emphasis on pastoral care.

After graduation, we put that training to work by becoming the pastoral care pastors at River Rock Church, in Colorado Springs.

In the fall of 2017, Bobbie and I began teaching a ministry elective at our alma mater on the ministry of helps entitled, *"Developing a Heart of a Servant."*

Satan tried to steal my voice, but I'm shouting it from the rooftops:

> ## *"I DIDN'T DIE. I LIVED! AND NOW I'M TELLING THE WORLD WHAT GOD DID."*
> – PSALM 118:17 MSG

The journey continues...

About the Author

Michael and his wife Bobbie have spent the last thirty years serving the Body of Christ in the area of the Ministry of Helps, seventeen of which were at Grace Church in Tulsa, Oklahoma under the leadership of Pastor Bob Yandian. Michael is a 1985 graduate of Victory Bible Institute, Tulsa, Oklahoma, and a 2017 graduate of Charis Bible College Woodland Park, Colorado. He was an Associate Pastor of Living Stone Church in Coweta, Oklahoma for seven years.

Bobbie is a 2010 graduate of the Grace School of Ministry in Tulsa, Oklahoma, and also graduated Charis Bible College in 2017. Michael and Bobbie have a call to use their thirty years' experience to teach the Body of Christ in the area of Helps Ministry and to conduct marriage seminars to help strengthen marriages.

They currently reside in Woodland Park, Colorado where they serve as the Pastoral Care Pastors of River Rock Church in Colorado Springs for Pastor's Rick and Joann McFarland. They also teach a class at their Alma Mater, Charis Bible College, on Ministry of Helps titled *Developing a Heart of a Servant.*

Made in United States
Troutdale, OR
08/06/2023

11857582R00066